Beginners Guide to Fishing

Copyright: February 22, 2010
All rights reserved by author

No reproduction in whole or in part of text or illustrations authorized without written consent of the author.

First Edition

Contents:

1. Brief Introduction to Fishing	Pg 3
2. Fish in General	Pg 7
3. The Different Fish	Pg 12
4. Lines and Hooks	Pg 31
5. Rods and Reels	Pg 36
6. What to Use for Bait	Pg 46
7. Artificial Lures	Pg 49
8. Bobbers, Sinkers, and Swivels	Pg 52
9. Gizmos, Gadgets, and Other Stuff	Pg 59
10. Safety	Pg 60
11. Angler's Responsibilities	Pg 61
12. Think, Think, Think	Pg 64

Chapter 1

Just a Brief Introduction!

I'm not surprised you want to fish! People have been fishing for a very, very long time. Before they wrote things in books or learned to build houses or even planted gardens, people learned how to fish. Even cave dwellers fished for their dinner.

Early anglers didn't have lines and hooks. They crouched on a log or rock, or stood very quietly in the water. They held a spear in their hand and waited patiently for a fish to swim into view. Then, *swish*, they speared their dinner – if they were both quick and accurate.

Then anglers noticed that in moving water, fish always faced into the current. Fish also tended to move up and down the streams in search of food or a place to lay their eggs. People built traps, like the fish trap shown below, to lay in narrow channels, so the fish would swim into them and be caught. But the traps were not very effective in the lakes and ponds where fish did not move through narrow passages between the rocks and currents.

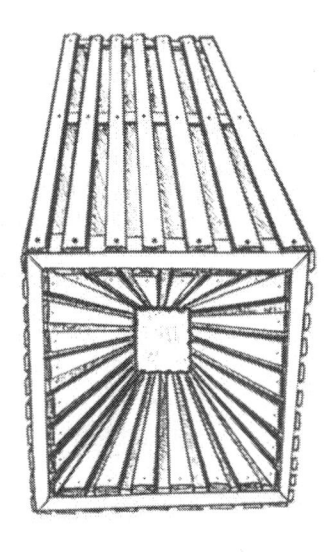

When people learned to make string and thin rope from plant fibers and the sinews of animals, anglers wove them into nets. Long nets were used to surround schools of fish in ponds, or stretched across rivers, so the fish would be forced to group up behind them as they traveled upstream. Then the anglers would spear the fish or scoop them out with long handled nets. Some nets were thrown over schools of fish, trapping them beneath.

Eventually, hooks were carved from animal bone and tied to the ends of small, strong strings. Some anglers simply jiggled the bare hooks in front of the fish until they became curious enough to strike. Some used small pieces of bait to entice the fish to swallow the hook. When people discovered how to shape metal, the hooks improved greatly.

Today, of course, we have metal fish hooks that are very small and thin but still very strong and sharp. Our lines are made of plastics and other artificial fibers. But one thing has not changed much at all. Just like the first anglers who speared their dinner, regardless of whether you use net, spear, trap or hook, if you want to catch fish, you need to know how they live!

What do they eat? What time of the day do they feed? Do they like sandy or rocky bottoms? Weeds or mud? Calm water or fast currents? Deep holes or shallow spots? The more you learn about the fish you want to catch, the better your chances of catching them. And that is what this book is for. This book is about thinking because that is the key to good fishing and the most important skill for the angler.

Your state conservation department is guaranteed to have great brochures on identifying the fish in your area, and giving you a good idea which species are found in which waters. And they're FREE. But be careful using color to identify fish, especially the trout. You need to learn about the markings and other traits that allow you to positively identify your catch.

Fish color can vary greatly from pond to pond and lake to lake. Brown trout that live in a pebble bottomed brook are likely to have bright coloring to make them blend in with the colorful bottom. But turn them loose to chase schools of smelt in a wide deep lake, and in no time at all they'll have far less color with just a dark top, and silvery sides and less bright spots. You see, color is actually a function of life in the fish. When they die it fades quickly. When they change environments, their color changes to help them be less visible. So a silver sided trout caught in the middle of the lake might not be a rainbow. It might be a brown, or a salmon. A bass in muddy waters might not have the dark, distinct markings on it's side. The bars of dark color will be faded, so the fish is not so visible in the murky water.

Chapter 2

Fish in General

So let's learn some important things about fish. First, we'll look at the things they have in common. Later, we'll look at the differences between the different kinds or "species" of fish.

The first thing to consider is that all fish need oxygen just as people do. Some species need lots, and others can live with only a little. But all fish get the oxygen by passing water over their gills which absorb the oxygen from the water and pass it into the blood. People have lungs instead of gills. When we breath, we move air in and out of our lungs. The lungs extract the oxygen from the air and pass it into our blood. So even though fish live in water, they breath oxygen too! The colder the water is, the more oxygen it can hold. The more movement there is on the surface of the water, the more oxygen gets mixed in. A fish that needs only a little oxygen may be comfortable in calm, warm water. A fish that needs lots of oxygen may need cool water, or water that is constantly tumbling, or a combination of the two.

When you watch a fish holding still in a tank or pond, and the gill plates are moving slowly in and out, you are seeing how the fish pumps water over its gills. In a current, the fish faces upstream so that the water can enter through the mouth and pass across the gills. This is one of the reasons fish generally face into the current unless they are actively swimming. Fish in moving water don't have to pump so hard to get the oxygen. A fish accomplishes the same thing by swimming.

The second thing to know is that each species likes a certain temperature range. They may survive in a very wide range– let's say from 33 degrees all the way up to 80 degrees. But the temperature range they like best may be only a few degrees – lets' say from 68 to 73 degrees. A fish may move into warmer water to have dinner, but it will usually go back to a more comfortable place as soon as it is through feeding. Some species like the water very cold or unusually warm, and others prefer it somewhere in between.

People have an advantage over fish when it comes to keeping a comfortable temperature. When people are too warm, they begin to perspire. The water evaporates on their skin and carries away some of the heat. If a person is too cold, the body begins to burn more fuel from the food they've eaten, and it helps warm the body up. But fish can do neither. Their bodies are made so that they take on the temperature of the water around them. If a fish is swimming in water that is only 40 degrees, the fish's body temperature will soon match the water. Their system slows when it's cold, so they don't move as quick and they don't need as much to eat. But even when it's really cold, such as in the Winter under the ice, they still must eat occasionally, and some fish, like yellow perch, don't seem to slow down much at all.

In order for a fish to maintain a comfortable temperature, the fish must move to colder or warmer water, or move into the shadows or out into the warm sunlight. Deep water is almost always cooler than the surface. Cold water is heavier, so it will sink down into the holes and channels. The deeper it is, the cooler it will stay because the sun is not reaching it to warm it. Moving water that passes in between steep cliffs or overhanging trees for a long stretch will tend to cool because it has not been exposed to sunlight. The longer it stays out of the sun the cooler it can become. Warm water is lighter than cold water, and so it floats to the surface. The sun penetrates this shallow water, helping to keep it warm, so the shallows and surface water tend to stay warmer. Water trapped in a wide pond and exposed to the sun day after day will become quite warm as the Summer goes on.

The third thing to keep in mind is that almost all fish are "carnivores." That means that they must eat other animals to fuel their bodies. Since no one is going to fix dinner for them, they must hunt for it or wait where the wind or current will carry dinner within easy reach. It is important to the fish to get the most food with the least effort. If they are expending more energy to capture their food than they are gaining from eating that food, they will starve to death. Imagine how long you would last if you had to walk many miles with a heavy pack on for every little thing you ate, and you had to do it 3 times a day! It wouldn't be long before you were too thin and weak to walk anymore, and then……So, it is important for the fish to find someplace to find food that does not make them exhausted just to catch it.

This is the other reason fish face upstream in moving water. They can watch for food approaching in the current and be ready to pounce on it. They wait in a calmer pocket in a depression on the bottom or behind a rock or log, and only have to fight the current for a few seconds when they dash out and grab the food. Fish will gather in groups where the feeding is very good. If the spot is also in their favorite temperature range, that is better still. The more closely a spot matches a fishes ideal temperature and food availability and cover, the more likely it is to hold fish. But even a place that is not so comfortable and has little cover will hold fish when the supper bell rings if food is concentrated there because fish have to eat to survive. The more they can get quickly and with less effort, the better off they are!

The fourth thing to remember is that fish are sensitive to light in varying degrees. On bright days, the fish are more visible from both in and out of the water, and many creatures like fish for dinner. Only sunfish and a few perch will stay near the surface in the bright sunlight in clear water. Even these fish tend to stay near to the shadows, bushes or weeds, so they have someplace to dash to and hide when they feel threatened. Some fish have become accustomed to living in the dark depths and they will come up to the shallows only after the sun has set. They will go back to the depths before morning. Other species may spend the day in the shade of weeds or lily pads. Still others may be comfortable in the shadows of a log or a sharp drop-off into the deeper water.

The fifth thing to think about is that each species of fish prefers to either stay alone or travel in small, medium or large groups called "schools." That preference can change as the individual fish gets bigger. If you catch one fish that travels in groups, you can probably catch more in that same spot. On the other hand, if it's the kind of fish that prefers to live alone, you will know to try fishing in a similar spot nearby. But the exact spot where you just caught your fish will most likely be empty until a new fish moves in. Keep the spot in mind though! On your next fishing rip, it will be time to try it again.

Fish tend to travel in groups because a school of predator fish can fan out and herd bait fish, making it easier to get a full belly (remember, more food + less energy to chase it = happier fish.) For smaller fish, schooling up also offers some protection. When a predator attacks a school of small fish all looking alike and all darting this way and that, it is very difficult to focus on just one and pursue it.

And sixth and last, it's obvious that fish have eyes and a nose, so they can see and smell. Did you know that they also hear very well? They can hear people walking on the banks, fish swimming in the distance, and frogs splashing in the dark because they have nerves that run down the side of their bodies that pick up vibrations in the water just as our ears pick them up in the air. However, water conducts sound better than air does. Largemouth Bass, for instance, can hear well enough to tell one kind of minnow from another as they swim by in the dark. This is how some species feed at night.

So, as you can see, exploring, learning about different fish, and thinking about what they need to be comfortable are very important to successful fishing – probably more important than your bait and fishing gear.

Chapter 3

The Different Fish

SUNFISH

The most noticeable fish in most areas are the sunfish. They are called many different names, and there are quite a few different kinds such as bluegills, longears, pumpkinseeds, and a number of other kinds. The drawing above is a bluegill, named for the very dark blue tab on the end of the gill plate. They are shaped alike and all have some things in common though. They like to bask in the sun (hence the name "sunfish,") and they prefer the shallower, calmer water, so they can often been seen from shore. They move about slowly near some kind of cover. Lily pads, weeds, brush, overhanging trees, docks, stumps, and even boulders or old rock pilings will do.

They eat almost anything that lives or falls in the water as long as it is small enough to swallow. You can often see them sampling items off the surface of calm water. What they don't find tasty, they simply spit back out. Bugs and minnows are their most common food.

Sunfish usually hang out in small groups of 3 to 5, and a particularly good spot may hold a dozen or more. But as with most fish, the biggest ones like to keep to themselves and stay out of sight in deeper water than the smaller ones.

YELLOW PERCH

These fish are found almost everywhere. They are very aggressive. They push right in and feed together in large or small groups whenever they have the opportunity. In shallow water, they are often seen racing past a few curious sunfish in order to grab the bait first.

Yellow perch can handle the warmer water too, but cold doesn't seem to bother them at all. They also like weeds, lily pads, and docks. But their favorite spot is near sunken brush or trees. When these things aren't available, they will stay near rocky bottoms or big boulders. If the brush or stumps are in deep water, they'll spend time there just as happily as they will in shallow water. Like the sunfish, perch eat bugs and minnows, but perch are better at chasing and catching minnows. Their mouth opens wider than a sunny's does, so they can swallow a minnow that a sunfish of the same size can't eat. Smaller perch are often found mixed in with sunfish near docks and brushy shorelines. They'll eat just about anything that passes by or falls in from the bushes or trees. Sometimes they move about in small groups, but more often they'll travel from one feeding spot to another in big schools. Even the very biggest perch like to stay in schools.

When a lot of food is available in fast water or heavy currents, the perch aren't afraid to move right in and feed. However, when the feeding is done, they're likely to move to a calmer spot. They are comfortable in a very wide temperature range. They will hang in the shallows in a warm summer pond, and they can be found in the deep colder waters at the ponds center on the same day. They are the most active fish under the ice in the winter, often keeping ice anglers busy when nothing else is biting. When you catch one perch, cast there again. There will almost certainly be more of them around.

CRAPPIES

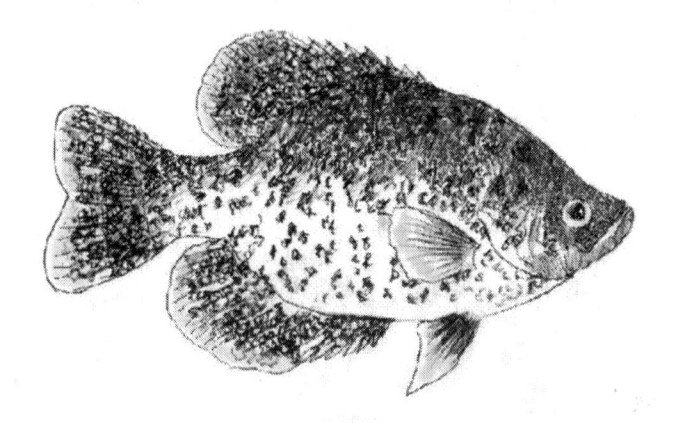

Sometimes called calico or strawberry bass, or 'paper mouth,' these fish are also fond of the warmer water. Their favorite cover is sunken brush and trees. People will often make their own brush piles by bundling brush and small trees together and sinking them just to attract these fish. If no brushy cover is available, look for them in the weeds or lily pads or under floating docks.

Although crappies are perfectly happy to munch on bugs, their very favorite meal is a minnow. Like the perch, their mouth opens wide, and they can swallow a pretty good sized minnow. They also travel in schools, and they don't mind the deeper water as long as there is cover and food available. Smaller crappies often stay with small groups of sunfish in the shallows. The bigger ones will be in separate schools in the deeper water or at least the deeper side of the brush or sunken trees. The bigger the crappie gets, the smaller the school will be, and the less likely you are to see it in the shallows.

They are often called "paper mouths" because their mouth is very easily torn, like paper, and it's very easy to tear a hook loose just by setting it too hard. Because of their big flat sides, they don't maneuver very well in heavy currents, but they will happily wait where the current slows down for food to be washed to them.

BULLHEADS AND CATFISH

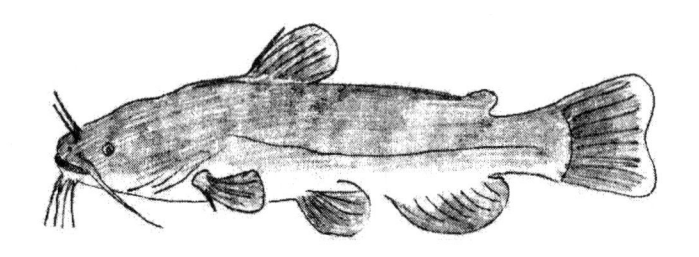

These fish are often considered the ugly ducklings of the fish family. The bullhead, pictured above, gets its name from its short, fat head, and the catfish family was named because of their "whiskers." The feelers that extend from each side of these fish do look like whiskers, but they are used to taste the waters and sediment on the bottom to find food. As you might guess then, these fish are primarily bottom feeders. They also like warm water.

Bullheads are a member of the catfish family that remain small in most waters. There are many more species of catfish though, and some of them grow to be very, very large. No matter which you fish for, remember that they feed primarily by smell. They cruise slowly about on the bottom, or they find a good spot on the bottom in a current and search for their food with their nose and feelers. They seem just as happy to eat something dead as alive, but they all enjoy worms.

Because they hunt by smell more than sight, anglers have invented all sorts of "stink baits" designed to attract them to the hook, and a chunk of liver is also a popular bait. They bite best in the dark, but most catfish will also take a bait during the day if it lands in their vicinity. If the water is very muddy or roily, so much the better for daytime fishing. Although they don't really travel in schools, a good feeding spot and comfortable conditions will attract large numbers of them. They don't mind weeds, but they're just as happy sitting on a mud or rock bottom with no real cover around.

Keep in mind when you catch one that there is a sharp spine that projects from the front of the dorsal fin and front of each pectoral fin (near the gills.) They are quite painful, so don't get jabbed.

ROCK BASS

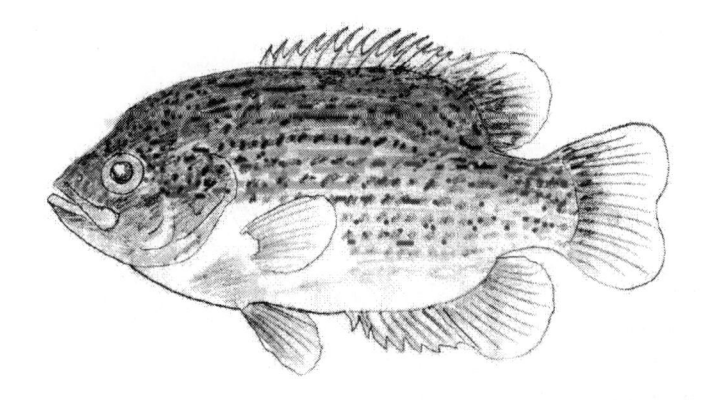

Rock bass are built a lot like the sunfish, but thicker and darker. They can be recognized by their dark brown color and red eyes. These fish prefer rocks to weeds, and they can be found in both swift and still water. They are very aggressive and eat almost anything. Like the perch and crappie, their mouth opens up wide enough to swallow a fat minnow. They don't often school up. Instead, you'll find them scattered along rocky areas looking for food.

They prefer warmer water and the calmer pockets of warm water streams and rivers. They are especially fond of hiding behind big boulders, between rocks in the current, or just to the side of a fast current in the calmer water.

All of these fish, sunnys, crappies, perch, catfish and rock bass are called "pan fish" because that is where they usually end up when caught. They don't generally have size limits under conservation laws, but many states have limits on how many you can keep. This limit is called a "bag limit" which comes from the days when fish were generally kept in a damp sack or bag when caught to keep them cool, prevent spoilage, and to carry them home.

The fish in the following section are referred to as "game fish" and are also generally good to eat. However, they are harder to catch than pan fish (because they are spookier,) and generally grow bigger and fight harder. They are usually subject to conservation laws that give both a size limit to ensure they live long enough to spawn at least once, and a bag limit to protect population levels.

BLACK BASS - Bass may be the most popular fish in the world. Almost everybody that fishes likes to catch bass. They grow much larger than the sunfish (who is a close relative) and bass often munch on the sunfish for dinner. There are two kinds of black bass that you are likely to catch, and each behaves differently.

LARGEMOUTH BASS

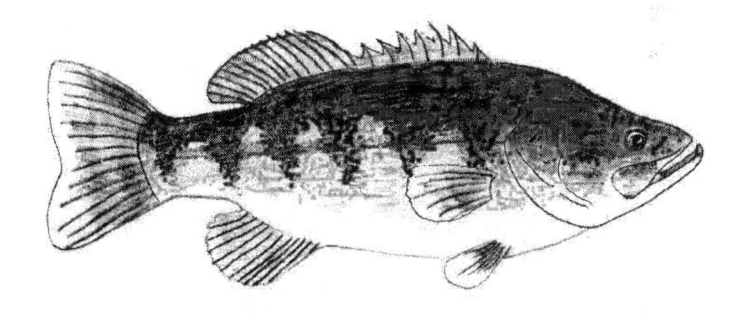

This is a very adaptable fish! In small lakes and rivers, they will look for a spot with cover. Weeds, lily pads, brush, sunken trees, overhanging limbs, jumbled rocks, docks, rafts, and even moored boats will do. In big lakes, these spots will hold bass too, but some bass will choose to travel in schools and chase schools of minnows out in the middle of the lake with no cover around. When they are closer to shore they tend to stay alone or in small groups of two or three. The bigger they get, the more likely they are to be alone.

The largemouth will eat just about anything that moves! Some of their favorite foods are other fish, frogs, bugs, and crawfish, but they seem to be just as willing to swallow small snakes, tiny turtles, and tadpoles. They have even been seen grabbing small birds that landed too close to the edge of a lily pad. In short, if it moves, a bass might just try it for dinner.

Because their mouth opens very wide, they are able to swallow things that the other fish in the pond can't. They like warm water but not as warm as the sunfish. If the water gets too warm, the sunnys and perch may stay in the shallow areas, but the bass will move to a deeper, shadier place until the water cools off in the evening. Then they will cruise back into the shallows and start hunting again. If the whole pond or river is shallow and warm, they won't be very active until the cool of evening or even the middle of the night when they use their hearing to hunt.

They prefer shadows to bright light, and they tend to avoid the current by hanging out along the sides in quiet pockets behind fallen logs or big rocks in creeks and rivers.

SMALLMOUTH BASS

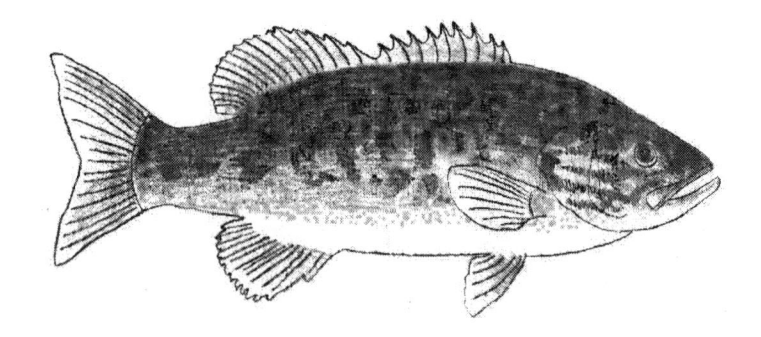

Don't let the name fool you! There is nothing small about the mouth of a smallmouth bass. It's only called "smallmouth" because their mouth is slightly smaller than their close relative, the largemouth. Smallmouths like a little cooler water than largemouths. They also like minnows and crawfish better than the wide range of meals the largemouth likes. They will, however, eat almost anything that moves when their favorites aren't readily available.

Because they like the water a little cooler than their largemouth cousins, in a lake or pond they will be found either in deeper water or close to where colder water flows in from a stream or river. In rivers, they will move right into the current and sit behind rocks, in deep pools and in the pockets and eddies along the sides.

They much prefer rocky areas to weeds, and they are most likely to be cruising a rock ledge or boulder strewn area, or a spot with a cobble or gravel bottom. They also like the shade when they can get it. The smallmouth is likely to travel in schools. You'll find the really big ones like to keep to themselves, cruising a good area and munching on whatever comes along. In the early morning and evening they may come to the surface or close into the shallows to feed. They also feed at night.

PICKEREL

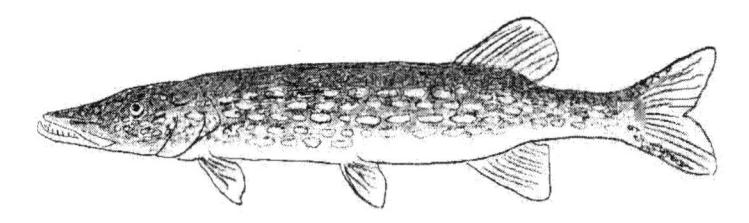

Pickerel are long, thin, green fish that travel alone and are almost always found in weeds (sometimes so thick that you'll wonder how they got in there.) When weeds and lily pads aren't available, try sunken logs and brush, but the thicker the cover the better!

They like warm shallow water and eat just about anything that moves near them. They also prefer shadows and feed best in the early morning and evening, but they are more willing to take a bait during the mid-day than bass are.

A small opening in a big weed patch or the very edge of thick lily pads is the perfect place to drop your bait. But when you land one, watch out for their TEETH! They are very, very sharp and there are plenty of them. Nobody reaches into a pickerel's mouth with bare hands twice! Use a pliers or a hook degorger to remove the hooks.

Pickerel hunt alone. But if the weeds are thick enough, and there's plenty of food, a few of them may be found lurking close together, looking for a dinner. They will take just about anything they can fit into their mouth, but minnows and frogs make up the bulk of their diet because those are common in the cover where the pickerel stay.

NORTHERN PIKE

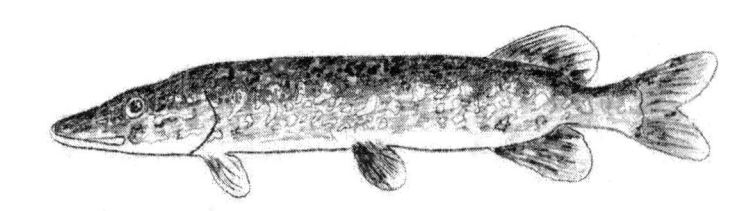

They're called "northern" pike because the northern half of the country and Canada is where they are most common. They like the colder water, but they can live in warmer rivers and lakes as well. Like their smaller cousins, the pickerel, these big hunters ambush their dinner from the weeds or from under sunken logs, and they hunt alone. And like their little cousins, they have a ferocious set of needle sharp teeth. Watch it when unhooking them! In faster moving water, they'll hang out in deep pools or even in the pockets of calm water behind logs or boulders. They love big, juicy minnows, but they have been known to eat a little of everything from frogs to snakes, and even swimming mice, muskrats and baby ducklings are on their menu. They grow big enough to eat good sized fish like the sunnys and perch and even small bass and trout. They don't mind shallow water or deep, as long as food and cover are available.

TROUT - Trout come in a variety of sizes, shapes, and colors. The different species have some very different habits, but they also share some important needs.

All trout need cold water with lots of oxygen. That means they'll only live in moving streams with clean, cold water, in ponds that have either cold springs or a cold feeder stream, or in a deep lake with a big pocket of cold water where they can take refuge from the summer heat.

Don't believe all that baloney about trout being smarter or harder to fool than other fish. Because the water they live in is almost always very clear, trout are very nervous creatures. They can be seen by all the creatures that would like to have trout for dinner, so they're always on the lookout for trouble. They can be very picky eaters, but the real reason some anglers don't catch many trout is because they're just too noisy or using too heavy a sinker, line and hook.

Remember that if you can see a trout camouflaged against the bottom, it can certainly see you silhouetted against the sky. The least little noise, the sight of a human, or the shadow of a passing bird may send trout scurrying under rocks or down to the bottom of a deep pool where they will stay motionless for a long time. This is especially true in streams where there isn't a lot of place for the fish to run and hide. They won't be back out to feed until they feel safe again. The more shallow and clear the water, the spookier the fish are.

But if you know what they're eating, and if you can move very quietly and stay out of sight, you can catch trout just like the more experienced anglers do!

BROOK TROUT

These trout got their name because they're common in small, cold brooks. In the very northern part of the country and in Canada, they're also found in ponds and lakes and rivers where the water stays cold even in the summer. They eat lots of very small insects that live or fall in the water, but they will also grab a small minnow if they don't have to chase it too far.

They like undercut banks, pockets under rocks, and the cool shadowy spots under logs and overhanging bushes. In ponds, they stay deep enough to be out of sight and like it under logs and bog mats. They also like it where a stream or spring brings cold water into the pond. In the morning and evening they sometimes scatter out over the surface of a pond to feed on small bugs. They can be difficult to catch at those times because they are focusing on a certain type of insect that is abundant. They are usually inactive at night.

Brookies don't like big chunks of food. They prefer little morsels, so keep your hooks and bait small. They are not aggressive, so when perch or even other species of trout are present, you won't find many brook trout around. Once a more aggressive species gets into a pond with brook trout, most of the brook trout are soon gone.

BROWN TROUT

The brown is probably the most common trout because it is the most adaptable. It can live in somewhat warmer water than other trout, it is more aggressive, it grows larger than the rainbows and brookies, and it competes with other species of fish for food and cover.

Browns like to sit under banks, logs, and overhanging bushes. The biggest ones always pick the best spots in the stream or pond to be safe and still have lots of food. Browns are just as fond of a fish dinner as they are of insects. When a big brown moves into a pool to live, most of the smaller fish move away - at least the smart ones do! In lakes, some will choose to travel in schools, feeding on minnows or big groups of insects when they're available.

But remember that they're just as spooky as the other trout. An oar banging on the boat - a dropped tackle box or rod - the sight of an angler waving a rod around on the bank - even heavy footsteps along the shore - will send them looking for cover.

Although they're more aggressive than the other trout, They're sometimes hardest to fool, especially with lures. But at other times they will tackle lures that you would normally use for bass, so don't be afraid to try different things when fishing for browns.

RAINBOW TROUT

Rainbows like the cold, faster water. They'll find a pocket right in the white water rapids and spend the day darting out into the current to grab passing bugs or minnows. Like the Brook trout, they need lots of oxygen, so cold, moving water, cold lakes, or ponds with cold inlets is where the best rainbow fishing will be. They also travel in schools in the deep lakes where they chase schools of bait fish or feed on insects near the surface or on the bottom. They prefer small and medium sized meals.

Rainbows also feed well at night. In lakes and ponds in particular, the best time to catch them is often after dark. Small minnows and night crawlers fished right on the bottom do well. They become more active earlier in the Spring than the other trout. They spawn very early in the Spring, and they can often be caught at the edge of the ice as it melts and breaks up.

Like most other species, the bigger the fish gets, the smaller the number of fish in the school. The biggest ones are most likely traveling alone.

LAKE TROUT

Lakers are the denizens of the deep. They like the deepest, coldest part of the lake. Unlike other trout, they're just as happy to eat a dead minnow as a live one. Because they live on or near the bottom in a sandy or rocky area, they don't often get insects for dinner, so their diet is almost entirely fish. They've got a big mouth, and they can swallow big fish. Suckers up to a foot long are a favorite bait of anglers trying to catch a big laker.

When the shallow water is cold in the early Spring and late Fall, they sometimes come into the shallows - but only after dark. They don't like the sunlight! They also like to stay together in schools, and even big lakers can be found living close together in deep holes.

When fishing bait for lakers, it's important to remember to give them time to swallow the bait. They usually grab the bait just in their jaws and then swim for some distance before taking the bait deeper into their mouth or throat. The suspense is nerve wracking when you see forty or fifty yards of line peeling off the reel before they stop to swallow the bait, and then resume swimming. When they've begun to move again is the time to let the line tighten and set the hook.

In northern lakes, lakers may cruise in water as shallow as four or five feet after dark in search of food. They're not fussy about what kind of minnow or cut bait they take, but they're not as likely to take worms or crawfish. By sun up, they'll be back in the deep. Stick with fish for best results. They also hit well on minnow imitating lures when you get them deep.

Well, those are the fish you are most likely to be fishing for, but there are many, many more swimming right along with them. Depending on where you live, walleyes, gar, suckers, drum, whitefish, eels, salmon, white perch, stripers, muskies and lots more might be on the list. The more you learn, the more exciting the fishing becomes and the better you're going to get at catching fish.

Remember that there are NO rules about fish that the fish don't break occasionally. Perhaps it's because they can't read and don't know about the rules. Don't be afraid to try something new. Experiment a little, and you'll learn a lot!

Also remember that fish don't get to pick where they're born any more than people do. A largemouth bass who is hatched in a deep, cold lake with very few weeds is going to adapt as best it can. It will catch crawfish and minnows instead of frogs and bugs. It will hang out near rocks or sharp drop-offs for cover instead of weeds and brush. It will do whatever it can to survive and be comfortable. A trout hatched in a pond with a deep, cold center and weedy shallows may have to travel into the shallows every day to feed, even if the water is warmer than the trout likes. If that's where the food is, the trout will feed in the shallows and then return to the comfort of the cooler, deeper water.

Learn about a few bodies of water by spending time on them. Learn the currents and pockets and the habits of the fish and insects there. Learn what you can about the water temperature and where springs or streams bring cold water into the lake. It all pays off in better fishing.

Chapter 4

Lines and Hooks

The single most important piece of tackle you will use is the one most often ignored. It's the simple little hook on the end of your line. If it is too big or too small for the fish you're after, it won't work very well. If it is so soft that it bends easily, a big fish may straighten it out and escape. If it is old and brittle, it may easily snap when a good fish makes a sudden surge or when you set the hook. Most importantly, if it is dull, it needs to be sharpened. Snagging on rocks will quickly take the very fine point off a hook. So will hanging in the garage or sitting in a damp tackle box, dragging along the bottom, or being pulled loose from snags. Yet, most anglers neglect to check the points of their hooks before fishing. When a hook is left anywhere damp, rust begins to work at the metal. It takes only a little rust on the finally ground point to dull it.

A good sharp hook is the surest way of hooking your fish and keeping it hooked. Every tackle store will have a hook hone of one sort or another on their shelves. If you can't locate one, even a small piece of emery paper will work. It usually only takes a few strokes to ensure a needle sharp point, and that is what you need.

Hooks come in more sizes and shapes than you can imagine, but for general purpose fishing, the only real decision you need to make is the size and whether or not you want the style called "Bait Holder."

Probably the most useful and popular size for pan fishing and trout fishing is a No.6. Even small trout and sunnys can get that into their mouth without a problem. If you happen to hook into a larger fish, a No.6 is large enough to have a good chance of hooking it and strong enough to keep them on the line. If you're intentionally fishing for bigger fish such as largemouths or lakers, a No.4 or even a No.2 may be a better choice, since those fish have a large mouth, and you'll probably be using a larger bait. The larger gap in the hook gives you a better chance of solidly hooking into the tough tissue of these fish without the big chunk of bait interfering.

The difference between a standard and baitholder hook is simply that barbs have been created on the shaft of the baitholder style. The barbs on the shaft prevent the bait from slipping down on the hook or falling off when a fish nibbles. The baitholder is not necessary when fishing live minnows since only the bend of the hook penetrates the baitfish. The little barbs make a big difference when fishing with baits such as grubs and worms though.

So what is best? After 50 years of fishing and trying many, many different kinds, I can only tell you this: They all work just fine if they're sharp and the right size for your intended fish.

A - Ring Eye
B - Turned Down Eye

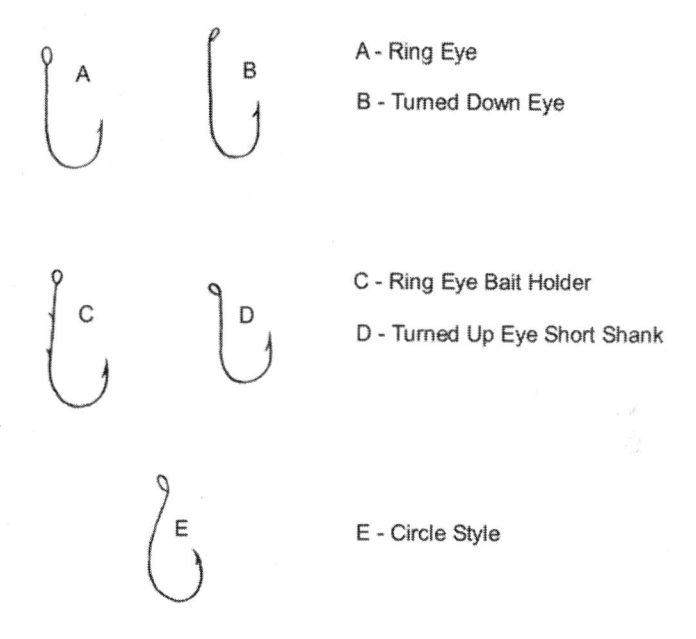

C - Ring Eye Bait Holder
D - Turned Up Eye Short Shank

E - Circle Style

The next most important item in your fishing outfit is the line. There are many different brands of line available. I know many anglers who have been fishing for years and have expensive rods and reels and beautiful boats. They have large tackle boxes crammed with the latest gimmicks and gizmos. They have the latest lures in a variety of sizes and colors. Yet, after investing all that money in tackle, they buy cheap line that is heavy and stiff. They don't often check their line to see if it has been nicked or become weak with age. When they loose a good fish, they can't understand what went wrong. When other anglers are catching fish and they aren't because their line is too heavy and stiff, they figure they're just unlucky. The fact is that their line is making it impossible for them to cast as far or as accurately as the other anglers. Their bait doesn't look or act natural in the water because it moves as if it were hooked to a stiff cable.

They'd be better off fishing with a simple cane pole and some good, light line. So would you. An expensive fishing outfit is no substitute for good basic tackle such as good line and sharp hooks.

Before you shop for line, you have to decide what strength or "pound test" you want. The strength of the lines are measured and labeled by how much pull it takes to break them. That pull is measured in pounds. Once the line has been tested, it is labeled with its **minimum** strength. So if the line is labeled 10 pound test, that means that it will take **at least** ten pounds of pull to break it. When you are shopping for line you might notice some lines claiming to be the "strongest" line in their pound test category. Naturally, you'll ask yourself, "How can one be any stronger than the other if they've both been tested and labeled as the same pound test?" And of course you're absolutely right. It's just an advertising and marketing trick. A line that is labeled 8 pound test but is stronger than other 8 pound test lines must be 9 pound, or 10 pound test. Remember that the pound test label is the minimum breaking strength. What you're really looking for is the line that is the strongest for it's thickness! That will be the one that gives you the best distance, the best accuracy, and will allow your bait to look most natural.

So, what pound test line are you going to do best with? As a rule of thumb, for sunnys, perch, and trout in streams, six pound test is plenty strong enough.

Many anglers only use four pound test, but you'll loose more lures and hooks to snags. If you're going to be fishing for bigger fish, or if you'll be casting near heavy weeds, brush, or rocks to snag on, eight or even ten pound test might be better. It's a trade-off between how far you can cast and how your bait behaves, or whether you need more strength to pull snags free or handle bigger fish in heavy cover.

No matter what pound test you choose though, you will need to check your line before and during fishing. The few feet down by the hook is the most important area to watch because it will receive the most rubbing during use. It should be very smooth to the touch. If it feels rough, or you see little nicks in it, cut off the bad section and re-tie your tackle. Exposure to sunlight and simple aging also breaks down the line and makes it weaker and more brittle. You'll be glad you took the time to check it when a big bass pushes past the sunnys, grabs your worm, and takes off for the far shore. If your line is old, worn, or frayed, the bass is going to leave you sitting on the dock with a great story about the one that got away!

Although it may seem like a waste and an unnecessary expense, it's best to completely replace your line at least every year. I know guides whose tackle is exposed to heavy use and sun almost every day. They change their lines monthly. Part of my Spring ritual each year when the snow begins to melt is to restring each of my reels with fresh line. When I head out for my first fishing trip, I know my line is going to do the job for me. Remember, all it takes is one little weak spot somewhere between you and the fish, and . . . . . .

Chapter 5

Rods and Reels

There are many kinds of rods and reels for sale. A simple cane pole that lets you swing your bait out from the shore or poke it back under the trees is plenty effective. A rod and reel to cast with simply saves you from moving around as much, and allows you to throw the bait to places you might not be able to reach with a cane pole.

When choosing a rod and reel, keep these things in mind. A rod is just a long stick that allows you to throw the bait further than you could with just your arm. The rod also keeps constant pressure on the fish, so the line has no slack in it, and the fish has to fight against the bend of the rod. That helps tire the fish out, so you can land it. It also serves as a 'shock absorber,' so you don't snap the line when you pull suddenly (which you shouldn't do) or when the fish pulls suddenly.

Rods - Rods come in an enormous variety of sizes, types, colors, and styles. They are made of many different materials or combinations of materials. The first consideration when choosing a rod is whether you will be fishing only with bait, only with lures, or both. A rod with "slow" action simply means that it bends a little over its entire length from the handle to the tip top. This helps keep you from snapping off bait with casts that are a little too fast and forceful. A "medium" action rod is built so that most of the bend occurs from about the middle of the rod up to the tip-top. This is a good choice if you are going to be casting both bait and lures. It helps stop you from making your cast too snappy for bait, but has enough snap to help you cast lures. A "fast" action rod is one that is fairly stiff until you come close to the tip top. The casts are very snappy, and it is good for lure casting, but unless you're careful, it will probably cause you to send part or all of a worm or minnow sailing out over the water without your hook attached.

Then, to complicate choices more, they come in ultra light, light, medium and heavy duty (and some in between.) Manufacturers use these as a guide for how heavy a lure or bait they handle best. They may even print a suggested lure weight range on the rods to help you make a good choice. For instance, the rod might say ½ through ¾ ounces. Does this mean you can't cast a lighter or heavier bait with it? No, but it will cast most easily and accurately with that weight range of lure.

The length of the rod does make some difference in how far you can cast, but the difference is not really as important as whether the rod is comfortable to you. A long rod may help you reach out over logs or brush, but a short rod might help you cast under low hanging bushes and docks, or help when you don't have much room to swing the rod when you cast.

Just as important as the right "action" on your rod is the eyes through which the line is constantly passing. If the eyes are just metal and the metal is cheap, the line will eventually wear grooves and rough spots in the eyes. Those spots will also fray and nick the line, and you know what that means! Ceramic eyes are more expensive, but they last much longer before they cause any damage to your line. Keep an eye on the wear of your rod's eyes. They are not difficult to replace, and a worn one will ruin your line and cost you fish.

Now, the rod must also be of a type to match your reel.

Reels - The two most important things about the reel you pick are how well it casts your line, and whether or not the drag on the reel is smooth and reliable. For beginning anglers, the casting is more important than the drag. As you become more experienced and learn to catch bigger fish, the drag will become more important.

If you are fishing for pan fish or smaller game fish such as stream trout, you may never need the drag on your reel. But a good drag is what allows an angler to catch a 10 pound bass on a 6 pound test line. The drag is a mechanical device that is adjustable. It allows the spool of your reel to slip, letting out a little line when a certain amount of pull occurs. When a big fish pulls hard, he may be pulling hard enough to break your line. If you have set the drag so that the spool slips and lets out a little line before it can break, then the fish just gains a little line, but it doesn't break off.

A 10 pound fish doesn't weigh 10 pounds when it's in the water. It really weighs almost nothing or it would sink to the bottom and starve to death. The fish adjusts whether it will sink or float by adjusting the amount of air in its bladder. It's a tiny balloon inside the fish that holds air so that the fish doesn't have to struggle to stay afloat. But fish are strong for their size, and a 10 pound fish can put more than 10 pounds of pull on your line by using its muscles to swim away from you when it's hooked. It goes right back to weighing 10 pounds when you lift it from the water. So lifting a big one without a net is a bad habit to get into.

If your drag is adjusted properly and operates smoothly, a fish cannot pull hard enough against the reel to make the line break. However, if you pull at the same time the fish is pulling, pressure may build up on the line faster than the drag can let line out. Then . . . . . .

There are four types of matched fishing outfits, all of which have certain benefits and drawbacks.

The first type is the spin-casting or push button outfit, which I highly recommend for beginning anglers, although they are not just for beginning anglers. The rod for this outfit has a pistol grip so that the rod can be held comfortably with the reel sitting on top of the rod when casting and retrieving. The eyes are comparatively small because the reel's nose cone opening is also small and the line doesn't form wide loops when you cast. The angler's thumb rests on a button or lever at the back of the reel during casting. The button is pushed and held while preparing to cast. It is released when the angler wants the line to be released.

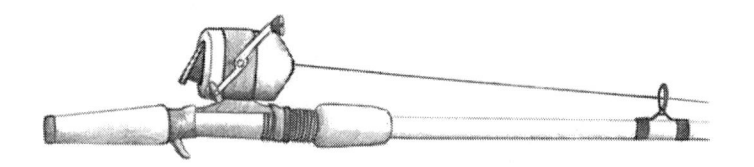

Because of the size and design of the reels, the drag on most of them is not quite as smooth and reliable as on spinning and bait casting reels. Additionally, the amount of line that the reels can hold is only about 100 yards. Despite these two drawbacks, this type of outfit is the easiest to learn to use well, and the drags on the more expensive models have improved greatly in recent years. A few minutes casting practice is usually enough to allow the angler to be fairly accurate. Within a few hours, most anglers can be very comfortable and accurate with this outfit. Just as importantly, if the line is kept from twisting, these reels are usually the most tangle free.

For most fishing, it is unnecessary to have more than 100 yards of line, (remember – that's a whole football field!) and a good quality push button reel can handle fish of 10 pounds or more despite the imperfections in the drag if you set it to let line out quite easily. The spin casting reel is also easy to clean and to repair. The mechanical workings are fairly simple and easily accessible. As with all reels and rods, you generally get what you pay for. A cheap plastic reel is quite likely to give you far more trouble and less enjoyment than a more expensive one. The line pickup on a cheap spin casting reel often wears the line. It is worthwhile to spend more money and get more hours of enjoyable fishing. A good spin casting reel costs about half of what a good spinning reel costs. It costs about 1/3 of what a good bait casting reel costs.

Overall it is the type most often recommended for starting anglers.

The next type of outfit to consider is the spinning rod and reel, or the "open face" reel as it is also called. The rod for a spinning outfit has a straight handle with no pistol grip. The reel hangs below the rod when casting and retrieving. The eyes on the spinning rod are much larger near the handle and taper up to a small tip top.

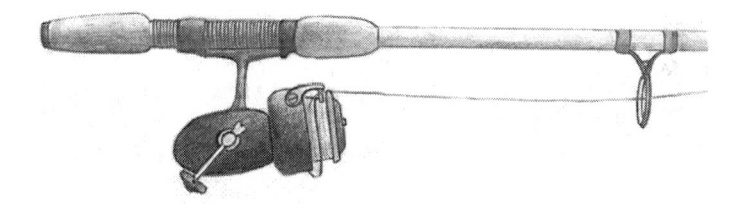

The larger eyes allow the line to coil off the spool in big loops with less friction. Spinning reels have no push button or nose cone over the spool of line. Instead, a spring loaded metal hoop called the "bail" is opened for casting, and closes itself when the reel handle is turned to retrieve the line. The line is held on your finger while preparing to cast and released when you want to the line to flow from the reel.

Because there is room for a larger drag plate on this type of reel, the drag is usually smoother and more reliable than on spin casting reels. There is also more room for line, and the average spinning reel may hold between 180 and 300 yards of line. This is certainly more than the average angler will ever need to catch and land a fish, even a trophy. However, it is more difficult to be very accurate with a spinning reel. More practice is required and until the angler is accustomed to using it properly, tangles in the reel are more likely than with a spin casting reel. However, the open face design will allow the angler to cast light lures and baits further and with less snap in the cast. This can be a great advantage when fishing streams for instance. The open spool also allows the angler to see when the line is twisting or looping, and when the line is getting too low on the spool. Because of the design of the reel, a faster rate of retrieve is possible which is an advantage when retrieving lures that require more speed, such as retrieving spinners downstream in a current.

As with spin casting reels, however, the cheap ones are more likely to break down, wear the line, and provide less enjoyment. When purchasing a spinning reel, look for a housing around the gear section that is very tight and fits without gaps or cracks showing. The pieces should have no rough ridges or edges. When cranking the reel, there should be no sloppiness; when the handle turns, so should the head. It should also be very easy to trigger the bail to close. If you have to ram the handle to get the bail closed, look for another model to buy.

There should be no sloppiness in the way the head fits the reel. Hold it in your hands and turn just the head with your fingers. If it feels loose, or you can hear any rough or grinding noises at all, look for another model. Repairing and cleaning spinning reels is a little more complicated, but once you learn how your model works, you can probably handle the job. This type of reel must be kept very clean and properly oiled in order to work well.

Bait casting outfits have been around longer than either of the other two types. While they are the favorite outfit for tournament bass and walleye anglers, they are not as easy to use, and probably not a great choice for the beginner doing a variety of fishing. The bait casting rod is built very much the same as the spin casting rod. It has a pistol grip and small eyes because the reel sets on top of the rod and the line spools out without any loops or coils.

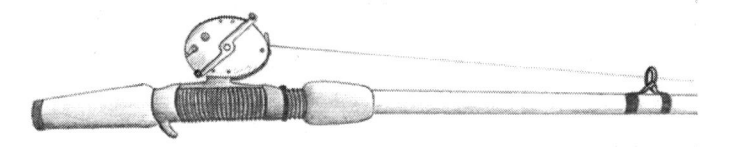

The bait casting reel is designed so that the angler has much more control over the cast and the retrieve, but it requires many hours of practice before an angler becomes accurate with them. Even though recent changes in their design have made them easier to use, they are still more likely to create tangles when they are adjusted for casting light lures or baits. However, they have a better drag system, and allow the angler to use the thumb to add drag directly to the spool when necessary. They are the preferred reel for trolling because of the added control when fighting a big fish and because of their high line capacity.

A cheap bait casting reel is far more trouble than it is worth, and a good bait casting reel is quite expensive. They do not cast light lures nearly as well as the other outfits. They are also more difficult to clean and repair because the mechanisms inside can be small and intricate. I recommend that you leave bait casting equipment until later in your angling career when you have a particular need for the benefits they offer, and you are better equipped to handle their problems.

The last type of outfit is the fly casting outfit. It is in a category of its own and it is difficult to compare to the other three. A fly fishing outfit is designed for use with an extremely light lure, one so light that a conventional spinning or spin casting outfit would only be able to cast it a few feet. Fly casting equipment uses a heavy plastic line that either floats or sinks. You are actually casting the heavy line, and the lure or bait is dragged along for the ride behind the heavy line. As a result, tiny flies that are close imitations of the real thing can be cast out 30 or more yards. The rod is long and flexible with very small eyes. The reel is only a spool to hold the line when not in use, or perhaps when playing a heavy fish. The larger reels for handling large freshwater and saltwater fish have an adjustable drag. The casting, retrieving, and application of drag on all models, however, can be done with the hands.

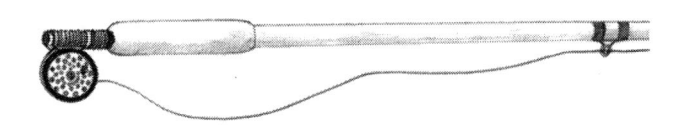

It is generally considered to be more fun to fight a fish on a fly rod than on other types of gear. However, much practice is needed to safely and accurately deliver the lure or bait. It is certainly not practical for casting minnows, crawfish, night crawlers, or any lures of any weight. However, it is the only practical way to deliver very small lures and tiny baits without the use of sinkers or bobbers. Fly fishing was

considered to be a very difficul[t]
fish for many years. Thankfully, t[...]
While I would encourage any angler t[o ...]
fish, I wouldn't suggest it as the main ch[oice ...]
beginning angler because it is very limiting.
also prove dangerous in a crowd because the f[ly]
bait will be sailing around on the end of 20 or 30
yards of line. Without proper caution, the hook can
easily end up in people instead of fish.

...for a particular fish is ...ame bait that worked ...day. The best bait for ...may not be very good ... There is always thinking to do and decisions to make. There are some good rules of thumb though.

When fishing for sunfish, perch, crappies, and rock bass, or for trout in brooks and streams, you still can't beat the old reliable worm. Almost all fish will take them. They're easy to find. They're easy to use. They keep well in a cool place. That all adds up to a pretty good choice for bait. That's probably why worms are the most commonly used bait among anglers all over the country.

Most days though, a small minnow will outfish a worm for crappies and perch, and they're usually more effective on trout in ponds and lakes than worms. A small or medium sized minnow is usually a better choice for bass and larger trout in lakes and ponds especially. And bigger minnows are usually best for really big bass and pike, and of course, lake trout.

But minnows are not always easy to come by when you want them, and they're not easy to keep alive either. Because of fish diseases being carried by baitfish, many states regulate where you can use minnows, and some even restrict their use to only the water they were captured in. Bait shops are being licensed and inspected to be sure they are not spreading fish diseases. That all adds up to more money per minnow and more expense for you.

So be sure to check the regulations for the state you're fishing in. Know what you can and can't do when capturing and using minnows and other baits. Sometimes in a shallow, weedy bay or small brook you can find all you need for a day's fishing. A wire minnow trap or small minnow net is not very expensive, but where do you keep them alive until you go fishing?

You'll need a bait bucket of some sort, an aerator or oxygen tablets, and a way to keep the water cool. Remember that cooler water holds more oxygen, and even minnows need to breath. If you can manage to trap or net a few right near your fishing spot, it's a much easier business.

Although worms and minnows are the most common baits, many others also work well. As a matter of fact, under the right conditions, some of these baits will work better.

Grasshoppers and crickets, lawn grubs and garden slugs all make very good baits for streams and for panfish of all sorts under all conditions. They even make special hooks and containers for fishing with crickets and grasshoppers because they are so popular in some areas.

Crawfish are excellent for bass and trout in large streams and some lakes or ponds. Use the smaller ones of about an inch to two for best results. They are very easy to keep alive by simply putting them in a little water or wet grass and keeping them out of the sun.

For catfish and bullheads, there are many commercial baits sold, but a plain old worm, a piece of raw chicken liver, or even a ball of bread dough wrapped around the hook works well. Salmon eggs, both real and artificial are also sold widely. They are fragile, however, and you'll need a small hook and a gentle cast. They are most often used for trout in moving water, but they are sometimes a good choice for panfish.

Chapter 7

Artificial Lures

The very easiest way to get two anglers into a discussion is to ask, "what is the best lure to use?" Even more than live bait, lures are effective one minute but not the next. They can be great on one lake and horrible at another only a mile away. There is a huge variety of lures available today, and most are effective at certain times under certain conditions. But the real answer to the question is, "the best lure is the one you fish with confidence."

There are a number of different categories of lures: **spinners - spoons - plugs - poppers - flies - jigs - plastic baits**. But some lures seem to be a cross between two of them.

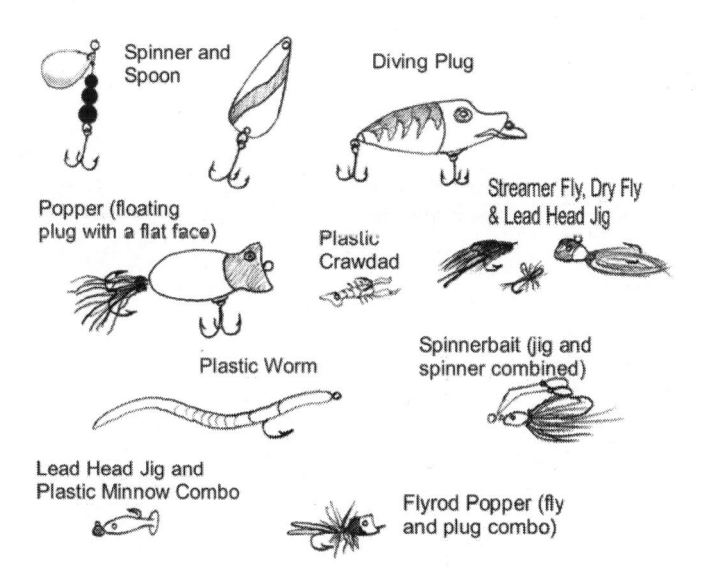

Spinner and Spoon

Diving Plug

Popper (floating plug with a flat face)

Plastic Crawdad

Streamer Fly, Dry Fly & Lead Head Jig

Plastic Worm

Spinnerbait (jig and spinner combined)

Lead Head Jig and Plastic Minnow Combo

Flyrod Popper (fly and plug combo)

The lure makers and tournament anglers divide these categories even further. (*Tournament fishing is what happens when you take an great pastime like fishing, add lots of noise, big engines, fast boats, and big money prizes, and turn it all into a floating circus.*) For instance, a plug that works by simply cranking on the reel handle is now referred to as a "crankbait." Long thin minnow imitations that only float and don't dive are now "stickbaits." Minnow imitations that have a small lip to pull them under when you retrieve are "shallow divers," and big lipped ones are "deep runners." You'll run across all sorts of interesting categories as you read more, mostly designed by marketing people to sell more lures, but all fall into the general categories listed above. Also keep in mind that most lures are really designed to catch anglers! Think before you spend money.

All lures fit specific situations, and the best way to choose them for your fishing area is to either ask someone with experience, or take a chance and try one out. A good lure is designed to act and look in a very specific way, which is an imitation of something fish eat. Because that can change from one body of water to another, the lure may or may not work well when you change locations. Some lures work well in many places because they are designed to imitate food found in many places. Most of the older anglers you meet will be happy to give advice to a new angler. As a matter of fact, it might be hard to get them to stop, so you can get back to fishing.

If I was forced to choose only one type of lure to fish with, the choice might surprise you. It is the least expensive, least exciting looking, and has absolutely no built-in action. It's the simple lead head jig. Because of the lead head, it's easy to cast. You can imitate almost any kind of fish food with it. You can add rubber baits or live bait to the hook. It can be fished shallow or deep, slow or fast. It's effective in moving water and still. And in really deep or very fast currents it may be the only lure that gets down to the pockets where the fish are. BUT, you-have to develop the skill of making it dance and wiggle and look good to the fish. Even the very cheapest jigs will catch fish once you learn how to use them. However, cheap plugs, spoons and spinners generally do not work very well at all.

Chapter 8

Bobbers, Sinkers, and Swivels

Bobbers serve two purposes. First, they hold your bait at a certain depth in the water. If the fish are swimming in 8 feet of water, you will catch more fish if your worm is dangling near 8 feet than if it is dangling at 2 feet. If you are fishing with a minnow or crawfish, letting either rest on a bottom with cover may result in it swimming under some weeds or crawling under a rock. Not only do the fish not see it, but it may result in a snag.

Secondly, the bobber indicates to the angler when something is nibbling or chasing the bait around. It also indicates when the fish has finally decided to grab the bait and take off. Try to choose a bobber that is big enough to float the bait, but not so big that the fish will feel a lot of resistance when it takes the bait. Most bobbers also add weight to the line and increase casting distance.

There many kinds of bobbers and sinkers, and more become available each year. The reason for so many different kinds is that each one does a certain job a little better than the others or suits a particular kind of fishing best. Pictured on the next page are just a very few examples.

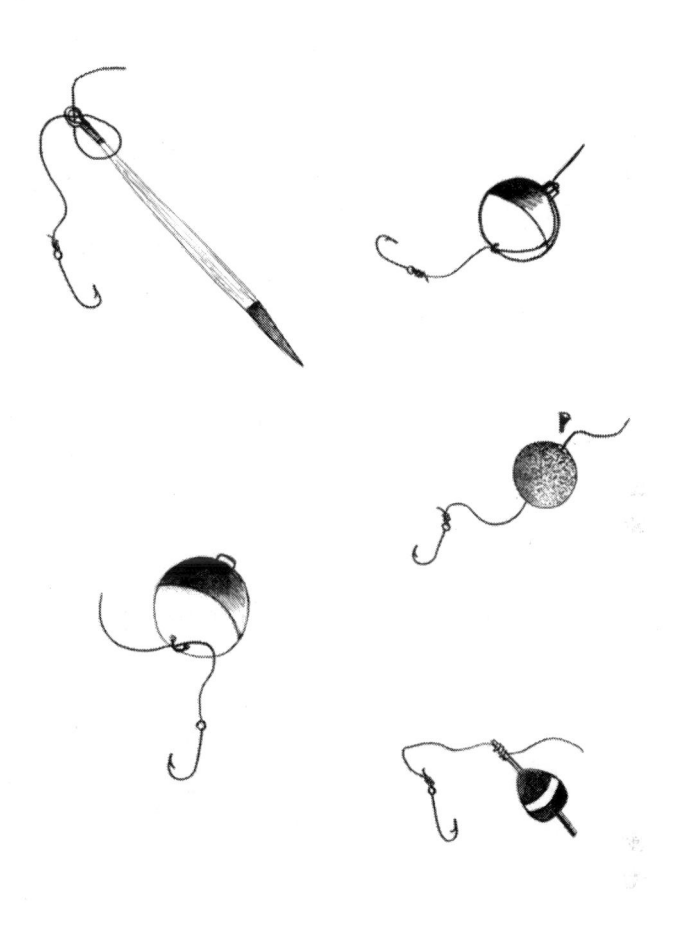

Bobbers have contrasting colors on them to make them easier to see when a fish moves them. In other words, it helps tip you off that something is 'nibbling' on the bait. Shape is important as well. The bobber at the bottom right will rest with the upper spike in the air and tapered shape down. It offers a little less resistance to the fish when it takes off with your bait. A simple round bobber offers more resistance, depending also on its size. Some fish (like trout) are spooky, and might drop the bait at the first sign of resistance. The porcupine quill (actually made from an African porcupine quill) at the top left will float only a small, light bait, but it will give almost no resistance when it goes under. However, it will not add any weight for casting distance, and even the weight of a small minnow or a really big night crawler can sink it. So once again, there is thinking to be done and choices made, depending on your tactics. One good rule of thumb is to use the smallest bobber needed to do the job you've chosen for it.

Now sinkers, on the other hand, are made for the opposite job. Sinkers are used to sink the bait, and keep it sunk. A minnow being fished on the bottom will try to find someplace to hide. The sinker keeps the bait in the spot where you have cast it. A lighter sinker gets bait down near rocks and pockets in moving water, but still allows it to drift along, passing as close as possible to fish waiting at feeding stations. Try not to use more weight than necessary to do the job you want.

The rigs illustrated below show just a few 3-way rigs used to keep bait on the bottom, or suspended just off the bottom. It is smart to use a much weaker line to connect the sinker to the swivel than the line to the hook. In that way, if the sinker snags up in brush or rocks, putting pressure on the line will break off only the weight, and let you retrieve the swivel with the bait and hook intact.

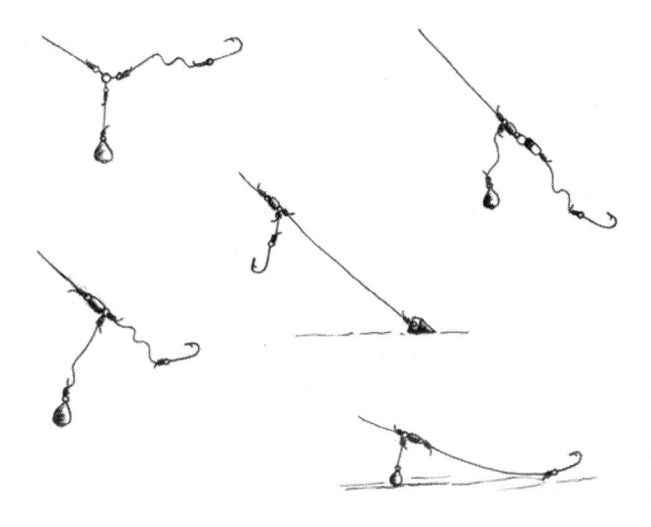

The swivel on these three way rigs is more about giving you a safe and easy way to join three lines together than it is about stopping twist. Knots to accomplish that job are tricky to master, and they'll weaken your line if tied improperly. You don't have to waste good money on expensive swivels for this, and they even make inexpensive 3 way swivels specifically for this purpose (top left, above).

Sinkers, like bobbers, come in an astounding variety of shapes and sizes because each does the job a little differently and probably just a little better under specific conditions. On the next page, you can see that the pyramid sinker is designed to not only give you additional weight, but to plow into sand and mud so the line will not be tossed around by the current or wave action. However, it is also shown in the rocks where it will usually snag, which can cause you to have to break off the line just to get your hook back and return to productive fishing. Below the pyramid sinker is a blade sinker, designed only to keep the bait deep in the water. Because of its shape, it does not hold very well in a current. However, it also has the advantage that it does not snag easily.

With or without bobber or sinker, the single biggest problem you will encounter is keeping your line from twisting. Once a line has been twisted from retrieving a lure or bait, snarls in the reel and a reduction in casting distance and accuracy always result. A twisted line is also less strong than an untwisted line.

If your lure or bait spins when lifted out of the water, or if little loops form in the line when there is no weight on it, it is time to straighten your line out. The best way in a moving stream or river is to let the line out downstream with absolutely nothing attached to it. In a boat, let it out behind the boat as you row or drift.

If you are at home or on a pond, try to find somewhere to pull the line off the reel and stretch it out over a long clean area of grass or sand with no weight on it. In any case, retrieve the line through two pinched fingers and the twists should work themselves out through the unweighted end of the line during the retrieve.

Consistent line twisting is cured by attaching a swivel. Spoons and spinners are certain to need one. A good one is worth the money because a cheap one seldom stops the problem. Snap swivels also make it easier to change lures, but can ruin the action on certain types of plugs and poppers. The sinkers and swivel rigs here only scratch the surface of the amazing variety of hardware available.

Some of the sinkers shown here are made so the line slips through them and they don't require a 3 way hookup, but that means the fish is likely to feel them when it grabs the bait. Go as light as you can no matter which type you use.

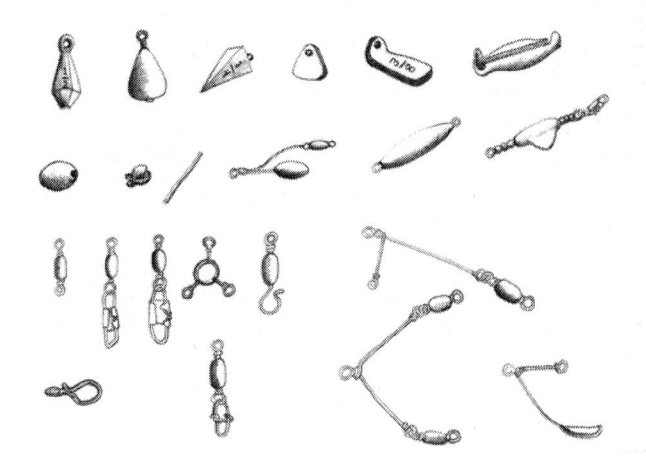

57

You also need good knots to tie on swivels or hooks. The simple overhand shoelace knot will cut your line strength about in half. Your 6 pound test becomes 3 pound test. Learn strong knots like the "improved cinch shown here," and others. There are small books dedicated to knots, and sports magazines often run articles on them. Practice them, so on a dark evening when you can barely see, and the bass are feeding all around, you can tie one in a hurry!

Tying the improved cinch knot

Start by pushing the line end through the eye. Then twist it around the main line at least 6 times.

Then go back through the loop that the twisting has formed at the eye.

Then push the end through the loop you just formed in the previous step.

Now moisten the knot to reduce friction, or heat will weaken the line. Slowly slide the twists toward the eye while pulling on the tag end until it forms a compact coil with the tag end sticking out. Cut the tag end close to the knot.

Chapter 9

Gizmos, Gadgets, and Other Stuff

Some other handy tools to have with you when you fish:

A pair of pliers is needed for removing hooks from toothy fish or from down in the throat of a fish that swallowed the bait. Medium sized needle nosed pliers work well for those jobs. A hook remover or "degorger" also works for removing hooks, and they come in a variety of designs.

A small container of band-aids is always handy for fixing small cuts and scrapes. I've even used them to hold the eyes on rods and fasten reels on when wrappings came loose or the reel seat broke.

A scaler is a good idea. It is both faster and safer than using a knife to rub off the scales from your catch.

Of course, a small sharp knife is needed to clean fish, and one with a few attachments such as tweezers and screwdriver blade can sometimes save a fishing trip when minor repairs have to be done on a reel or other piece of tackle. An old design still available has a blade, fish scaler, and hook degorger built right in.

You will also find that nail clippers are very handy for clipping off the tag ends of line when changing lures, hooks, or swivels.

Chapter 10

Safety

How about safety? Do you know how to help a friend who falls in the water or gets hurt while fishing? Do you know how to help yourself and how to avoid getting into a bad situation in the first place? There are many good guides to first aid that can be purchased or borrowed. I never go on a fishing trip without a first aid kit in my box. Chances are that if you are spending time with sharp hooks, knives, boats, slippery rocks, docks, and other anglers, sooner or later you'll encounter the need to help someone or yourself. Be a responsible angler, and be prepared.

The two most important things to remember are simple and will prevent most accidents. First, if you're there to fish, then fish. If you want to horse around, go home or to a playground. It is very easy to get hurt or put someone in danger around water. Secondly, always know where your hook is and the position of anyone else nearby. The length of your arm, the length of your pole, and the line hanging off the end can reach six to 10 feet. Measure a 20 foot circle and stand in the middle, and you'll see just how dangerous a little carelessness can be.

Sometimes a hook can be removed with only a little discomfort and trouble. Just as often it means a trip to the emergency room where a doctor has to cut the hook out, stitch up the cut, and disinfect the wound. It can be painful and expensive.

Chapter 11

Angler's Responsibilities

Along with all the fun, you also take on quite a bit of responsibility when you become an angler. You take on the responsibility for your own safety. You also have a responsibility not to endanger the other anglers around you.

You take on the responsibility to keep the areas you fish clean and enjoyable for both the area's wildlife and other anglers. That includes not spreading fish diseases through improper bait use, and not introducing fish species that might ruin the fishing in the future. You can do that simply by using the wrong type of minnow in a brook trout pond, or stocking pan fish somewhere because you think you'll improve the fishing. Remember that the balance in a lake, pond, or stream can be destroyed very easily, and the fishing could be ruined forever as a result!

If you're fishing on private property, you have a responsibility to the folks who own the property not to litter or damage things, or leave gates open that were closed when you entered.

Remember that the fishing line you leave laying around can be deadly to birds and animals that prowl the shores in search of food. Once they become entangled in the line, they may no longer be able to hunt, and they will starve to death.

Most importantly, don't be afraid to clean up after some slob who doesn't care about others or the environment, and don't add to the problem by becoming a slob. Many good fishing holes have been posted with "No Trespassing" because of litter bugs and people who wouldn't take their responsibilities seriously. Don't be part of the problem, be part of the solution.

Lastly, you have a responsibility to the wildlife around you, including the fish you catch. Every state has fishing regulations designed to ensure good fishing for everyone. If your fishing is going to be as good tomorrow as it is today, it will require the cooperation of every angler. Conservation laws were designed for good reasons, and while they can be annoying when they stop you from doing something you'd like to do, they are important to ensure good fishing is not ruined. Obey the laws, and encourage others to do the same.

So what happens when you see a good fishing spot, but there are posted signs? Have you considered contacting the owner of the property, introducing yourself, and asking permission to fish there. People generally post their property to stop the slobs from ruining it. When you show good manners by respecting their signs and asking permission, and then show respect for their property, many owners will allow you to fish even though it's posted.

Does that permission include a friend? You need to be sure. If that's what you have in mind, you better ask. And if you bring a friend who causes a problem, who do you think will be held responsible? Something to think about when you choose your friends for fishing is whether or not their behavior is acceptable because it will probably affect peoples' opinion of you as well.

Do you show courtesy to other anglers? How would you feel if you're fishing, and somebody barges in and plops down right next to you and casts out near your line? Or comes down to the shore where you're fishing and starts skipping stones? Or charges down to the bank of a stream right where you're casting for trout? Don't do things to others that you don't want done to you......

While there are plenty of fish for anglers to take home for dinner, there aren't enough fish to waste. Nothing is sadder than seeing a stringer of fish end up in the garbage can because they were left too long in the sun and spoiled. If you're taking home your fish just to show off your skill, you're killing animals for a very selfish reason. A fish that is released uninjured can be caught again and can spawn other fish so that everyone can enjoy good fishing.

Chapter 12

Think, think, think

Well, that's quite a lot of information to digest isn't it? But that's really what successful fishing is all about – using information and thinking!

Let's say you want to catch a trout. Where do you start? Well, obviously, you need either a deep lake or pond with cold water, or you need moving water that remains cool even in the summer. You need to be there when the fish are actively feeding for best results, which means noon time on a sunny day is not likely to be as good as early morning or the evening hours. You need bait suitable for the trout you're after, and tackle that can get that bait in front of the trout without spooking them.

Sometimes you don't get to choose where you're fishing. You go on vacation, and the pond across from your cabin is shallow and warm, and has big weed beds on both ends. You don't have a boat, so you can't explore the center. Would you gear up for Brook Trout? Not Likely! After all you've learned, you know that the pond most likely holds warm water species like sunnys, perch, bass, pickerel, and maybe bullheads and catfish. So where do you go and what do you use? There's weed cover to be explored. You should cruise around looking for sunken trees, brush piles, stumps, ledges, or anything else that will serve as cover for these fish. You then have to decide to use smaller baits for the smaller fish, or take your chances on bigger baits and bigger fish even though there will be fewer of them. You can watch the surface and look for feeding activity or schools of minnows. In short, you have to solve the puzzle of what's there and how best to catch it.

Perhaps you're going boating on a big lake that you don't know much about. How about asking other anglers or stopping in at the sporting goods store, or even the local police station? There's almost always somebody at the local police station that fishes. If not, they'll know who to send you to for good fishing information.

But even without help, you know what you're looking for. Sharp drop offs, channels, or ledges are a good start. Weed beds, rushes, and lily pads are visible items, but how do you find the invisible cover under water? The simplest method is to be observant. How does the land around the lake look? Are there places where the land slopes very slowly down into the lake? Chances are it continues pretty much under the water as it does on the shore. So when you find somewhere that drops down very sharply into the lake with stone cliffs and loose boulders, chances are it will continue as a drop off into deeper water, with stones on the bottom, and maybe some trout or smallmouth bass hanging out?

Another simple method is to use a sinker and hand line. Simply lower it over the side to find out how deep the water is. Bounce it gently off the bottom as you move, and when you find some place that suddenly gets deeper, you've just discovered a ledge!

How about your approach to the shore of that shallow, crystal clear brook, or the very quiet rock bottomed pond with no weeds and clear water. The fish are going to be spooky because they can be easily seen, and they can easily see the predators overhead and on the shore. Their only protection is to run from trouble. Do you stand upright in the sunlight and wave your arms and rod around? Do you clomp around on the shore and drop your tackle box, sending out an alarm for every fish in the neighborhood? Not if you're smart. Why not try crouching low, keeping bushes on the shoreline between you and the fish where you can, and walking very, very softly. Cast from as far away from your intended target as possible.

Will you walk downstream so that every fish there is looking upstream at you as you approach, or will you sneak upstream and fish for them from behind, where they have a blind spot? You'll get much better results when you think about your approach.

How about sitting in the boat, and flipping open the lid of your tackle box, so it bangs on the seat, dropping the oars against the side of the boat, and dropping your anchor over the side right where you intend to fish? Now if you're thinking, you know that none of those things is a good idea, but anglers do it every day without thinking, and then they wonder why the fishing is so slow!

Did you ever watch boat anglers in a creek. They move along the creek, casting toward shore. They work the edges of the weeds or end of the fallen trees, and in and out of the rocks. Now watch the shore anglers. The walk up to the shore and cast out to where the boats would be. Fish like cover. If you sneak quietly up to a shore line, you'll find you might not have to reach the middle of the creek to find fish. They may be sitting right along the shore, at least until you scare them off! Think about it before you plop down and cast way out there.....

Remember that where you live may be a different climate than where you're fishing. If you live in New Jersey, and you're fishing in Canada, the pond that looks just like the one in your neighborhood is going to be colder even in the Summer, and the fish are going to be used to colder water. The Winter is longer and Summer is cooler, so even in Summer the water is not likely to warm up as much as the water in New Jersey. On the other hand, if you're fishing in Georgia, you should expect that even the big bodies of water are going to get warmer than you're used to. The Winters there are shorter and warmer, and the Summers are longer and hotter. The fish will be acclimated to what they grow up in. What a Canadian or Maine Smallmouth considers warm could be colder than the coldest water a Mississippi or Georgia bass ever sees.....You have to adjust your thinking to succeed.

What are you going to wear fishing? Will you have on bright red hat and yellow shirt? If you're going to be standing on the shore of a shallow, clear brook, you might just as well call ahead and warn all the trout to dive for cover, because you're on your way to fish!

Stay alert, watch what's happening around you, and learn something new from every fishing trip. And think, think, think. In no time at all, you'll be a seasoned and successful angler. But keep in mind

that you're not the only creature who wants to fish. Cut up your wasted fish line and take it home for the garbage. Enjoy your fishing, and let others enjoy theirs too.

Good luck.

Made in the USA
Lexington, KY
28 May 2018